WE ARE OUR ANCESTORS' KEEPERS

WE ARE OUR ANCESTORS' KEEPERS

Melanated Edition

CHARLES 3X ALEXANDER

Illustrated by Adin Parker

ELITE 8 BOOK PUBLISHING
San Diego, California

WE ARE OUR ANCESTORS' KEEPERS
Melanated Edition
Published by
Elite 8 Book Publishing
San Diego, California
Email: weareourancestorskeepers@gmail.com
www.weareourancestorskeepers.com

Publisher: Charles 3X Alexander
Writers: Bianca Lewis, Ciara Guss,
Katinka Kepler, Caisha Frierson Muhammad, Ninus Malan, Nuri Muhammad
Editors: Maria Muhammad, Pamela King
Artist: Adin Parker
Project Manager: Lan Jefferson
Elite 8 Administration: Akilah Shaheed, Jeffrey Jones, Jordan Harrison & Rachel Evans
Book Packager: Yvonne Rose/qualitypress.info

ALL RIGHTS RESERVED

No part of this book may be reproduced or transmitted in any form or by any means – electronic or mechanical, including photocopying, recording or by any information storage and retrieved system without written permission from the author, except for the inclusion of brief quotations in a review.

Elite 8 books are available at special discounts for bulk purchases, sales promotions, fund raising or educational purposes.

© Copyright 2018 by Charles 3X Alexander

PAPERBACK ISBN #: 978-1-937269-77-7

HARDCOVER ISBN # 978-1-937269-85-2

EBOOK ISBN #: 978-1-937269-84-5

Library of Congress Control Number: 2017919621

DEDICATION

To all the Melanated Children
Around the World.

Table of Contents

PART ONE -- 1

Great Melanated Heroes & Sheroes from Ancient Times to the Middle Ages ---------- 1

   The Story of Imhotep -- 2

   The Story of Nefertiti --- 4

   The Story of Hannibal -- 6

   The Story of Cleopatra --- 8

   The Story of King Alfonso I -- 10

   The Story of Candace --- 12

   The Story of Mansa Musa -- 14

   The Story of Makeda --- 16

   The Story of Yasuke Oda Nobunaga -- 18

   The Story of Amina --- 20

   The Story of Antar the Arabian Negro Warrior ------------------------------ 22

   The Story of Yaa Asantewaa --- 24

   The Story of Shaka Zulu --- 26

   The Story of Nzinga Mbande -- 28

PART TWO -- 31

Great Melanated Heroes & Sheroes in the United States from the 17th Century to Present Times -- 31

   The Story of Toussaint Louverture --- 32

   The Story of Bass Reeves -- 34

The Story of Madam C.J. Walker ---------- 36

The Story of Dr. Mae Jemison ---------- 38

The Story of George Washington Carver ---------- 40

The Story of Charles Drew ---------- 42

The Story of Oprah Winfrey ---------- 44

The Story of Muhammad Ali ---------- 46

The Story of Serena and Venus Williams ---------- 48

The Story of Nick Cannon ---------- 50

The Story of Colin Kaepernick ---------- 52

The Story of Marilyn Mosby ---------- 54

The Story of Aaron McGruder ---------- 56

The Story of Misty Copeland ---------- 58

The Story of Beyoncé Knowles ---------- 60

The Story of Simone Biles ---------- 62

The Story of Michelle Obama ---------- 64

The Story of Barack Obama ---------- 66

PART THREE ---------- 69

We are Our Ancestors' Keepers: "Knowledge is Power" Quiz ---------- 69

Acknowledgements ---------- 105

About the Author ---------- 111

PART ONE

Great Melanated Heroes & Sheroes from Ancient Times to the Middle Ages

The Story of Imhotep

The world's first recorded genius is a man named Imhotep. Our young prince of peace was an architect, astronomer, philosopher, poet, father, and physician of medicine. Though Aristotle, Plato, Socrates, and Thales are well-known, this brilliant man lived before those individuals ever existed. Thales lived in 600 B.C., where he was recorded saying to his students, "If you desire to master the mind, master philosophy." To do this, he advised them to go where he went to study, the land of Egypt. Why? Well, in 2300 B.C., there was a philosopher named Imhotep. There was a doctor named Imhotep. There was an architect by the name of Imhotep that had mastered high science and math and had become so well-versed in the power and use of the brain, that he developed an architectural blueprint for the greatest of all structures known to the world; the pyramids! Here you have a black prince that builds a pyramid 451 feet tall and digs into the earth 451 feet deep. He uses one million blocks of granite. And covers thirteen acres. And each block weighs 3 1/2 tons. Yet, he had no hydraulic system. Yet, he had no special lifters. Yet, he didn't have a crane to work with. But, a man stacked 1 million blocks, 3 1/2 tons apiece 451feet high and deep; 13 acres. With no equipment. Tell me that man wasn't a master mathematician. Tell me he was a master philosopher. Tell me he wasn't a master builder. A black prince named Imhotep. And every angle is mathematically precise. Every corner is set to the square inch. How could a prince do it unless he had mastery over the power of the Black Mind. The same genius that lies in him, lies within all people that are enriched with melanin.

The Story of Nefertiti

Mystery surrounded this powerful princess in ancient Egypt. She's known as the most beautiful woman in the world and ruler of the Nile River. Nefertiti loved the beauty that her melanin possessed. Every chance the princess had, she celebrated herself! Her swan-like neck was draped in gold beads called nefer which was said to be worn on her neck due to the similarities in her name. The princess may have even made the first line of makeup out of Galena plants. Her birth would be considered magical. She gifted the world with her presence in 1317 B.C. in Thebes, Egypt. The regal young princess grew into womanhood and became the wife of Egyptian Pharaoh Akhenaten in 1357 B.C. Her husband ruled from 1353 B.C. to 1336 B.C. Legend says the princess sat equally to her husband on the throne. The married couple conceived six daughters together. Known to be the Daughter of Pharaoh (Ay), Nefertiti became the most recognized Egyptian woman. However, many historians have tried to completely write her out of history because it's rumored that Nefertiti was King Tut's mother. The memory of Nefertiti reappeared when a sculpture of the upper part of her body was found in a rundown shop in Amarna, Egypt in 1912. Since then, she's become one of the most revered and copied historical figures in the world.

The Story of Hannibal

Young Hannibal is known as the greatest general and military strategist who ever lived. He was born in 247 B.C.E. When Hannibal was just a boy, he developed a fascination with other tribes' styles of fighting and defending territories. He knew one day he would bring all the tribes together for one goal: to fight for Africa. The young prince prepared himself to overthrow the Roman Empire. Hannibal gained the courage to weigh the risks and marched his army along with African war elephants over the Alps. They defeated the enemies of Africa by surprising them with strategic military tactics that they had never encountered in war. He conquered Northern Italy and part of France. His tribes captured troops on the battlefield and forced them to join his army. His dream came true. He used all his enemies' ways of fighting to defeat them. Hannibal's skills are studied in many military schools today, as his legacy lives on forever.

The Story of Cleopatra

Cleopatra was 18-years-old when she began to rule an empire in Ancient Egypt for thirty years. She shared the throne with her two younger brothers, and later with her son. Along with being a great beauty, she proved to be the strongest and most intelligent leader amongst her siblings. Cleopatra could speak many different languages, which gave her a favored position in leadership. Ptolemy XIII, her 10-year-old brother, betrayed her due to his jealousy and ill-advice, and forced her out of Egypt. The princess escaped to Syria, and upon her brother's death, she returned to her rightful place on her throne. However, during her most successful role as princess with her son by her side, tragedy struck in the form of natural disasters, floods, and hunger, causing desperate times and a need to seek help. Rome was her help. Caesar of Rome filled that role of savior, before his death. Shortly after, Rome was split into two parts between Marc Anthony and Octavian. Marc Anthony was quickly tempted by the charm and beauty of Cleopatra and promised to protect her Egyptian crown. The Goddess left Rome and returned to Egypt with Marc Anthony close behind her. Later, she gave birth to two more sons by Marc Anthony. Octavian was none too pleased by the turn of events and war broke out, during which both Marc and Cleopatra's empires were captured. Cleopatra will always be remembered as the great beauty with a shrewd political mind and intelligence.

The Story of King Alfonso I

Alfonso was born in 1506 with special powers that allowed him to see and do things that most princes were not able to do. He had the gift to unify the Kingdom Of Kongo. Fully equipped with advanced knowledge and technology, Alfonso had fun working with the elders as they taught him the ways of the past and how he must think about his people before himself. As a great leader, he adopted incredible skills and understood the concept of protecting his people's future. Well, that day finally came, when the enemies were plotting to overthrow his people and it was up to his teachings to make him fruitful and victorious. Alfonso went down in history as the first ruler to resist the most despicable act ever known to man: the European slave trade.

The Story of Candace

The princess was a woman of much strength, and her name fit her well. Candace, which means "Great Woman," served as a ruler of Ethiopia, the Kingdom "Kush" also known as Nubia. This woman demanded respect through the way she carried herself and led her army into battle. Candace's incredible military prowess forced her enemies to stay sharp. When preparing for war, Candace provided her military with supplies and weapons to fight for the long haul. In 24 B.C.E., the princess announced the war against the Romans, which lasted for 1250 years. The battle ended after much bloodshed in 350 C.E. The Kingdom of Kush was victorious, and the civilization flourished, making it one of the most uniquely created cultures under Candace's leadership. Sadly, not much else is recorded during her reign over the Kush Empire, but what is known of her life story is passed down through legends which rave about the fearlessly and athletically built woman who was blind in her right eye and defeated Alexander the Great. Despite many personal disabilities and unfavorable circumstances, the princess overcame her obstacles and led her army and people into success.

The Story of Mansa Musa

As the prince of Mali, Mansa Musa was a scholar and wise ruler. He was known for being brilliant and original. In 1324, he led his people from Timbuktu to Mecca. His caravan consisted of 72,000 people, who he led safely across the Sahara Desert and back, for a total distance of 6,496 miles. When the young prince entered Mecca, four young homeless friends were sharing a piece of bread. Remembering what his teacher always taught him: "Want for your brother what you want for yourself," the young prince ordered his men to stack four stacks of gold twice these young men's heights so that their house may be built on solid ground, and their families may one day return this favor. He gained the respect of scholars and traders all over the world and made Mali one of the most influential and wealthiest empires in the world. The empire at this time had one of the most prestigious universities in Timbuktu.

The Story of Makeda

This princess was extraordinary. Makeda was predicted as a princess whose name would live on forever. As a young princess, she obtained knowledge of nature, mathematics, and music. A young king by the name of Solomon heard the Kingdom of Sheba had been the only empire on earth, not under his control. This news made the King interested in the Ethiopian Empire. Princess Makeda was one of the richest, mightiest, and most beautiful princesses throughout the land. King Solomon sent his fastest messenger to the land of Sheba with a letter commanding the princess to be brought to him under his rule. In return, Princess Makeda sent King Solomon ships loaded with precious gifts including spices and gold equal to today's standard of $3,500,000. She also included precious stones and beautiful wood, proving to the Great King that she was just fine on her own! When Princess Makeda finally arrived in Jerusalem, she arrived with a caravan of camels. King Solomon and his people were amazed by the great princess and her beautiful people, and he went to great lengths to accommodate her every need. A unique apartment was built for her stay in, while visiting his land. She also consumed the best foods and wore the finest clothing. They played games together, traded knowledge and enjoyed each other's company. The King admired Princess Makeda, as she admired him, too. They had a child together, a son named Ebna Hakim. King Solomon tried his best to keep Ebna Hakim in Jerusalem because his goal was to make him ruler of his empire, but the prince returned to rule Ethiopia where his mother and many women before him ruled. Eventually, Ebna Hakim took on the name "Menilek I"; making him the first Emperor of Ethiopia.

The Story of Yasuke Oda Nobunaga

This is the story about a young African warrior who became the first African samurai. The day young Yasuke arrived in Japan around 1579, his presence drew sizable attention from people. Some even fell trying to see his exotic appearance! When the commander, Oda Nobunaga, heard of the man, he immediately asked to see this young African warrior. "They say, 'He was a healthy good-looking man,'" he said. Yasuke's strength was greater than ten men and he could speak several languages, including Japanese. Commander Nobunaga became so impressed by Yasuke that he invited him to become a Samurai class member, a rare honor among foreigners. One day, enemies called Mitsuhides, attacked and defeated Commander Nobunaga at a place called Honnoji. With his determination to not give up, Yasuke fought his way to Nobunaga's side. He tried with all his power, to get Nobunaga to Nijo Castle. Unfortunately, their party was captured by Akechi troops, halfway through the journey. Yasuke fought bravely to protect Commander Nobunaga. Even when he was captured, he refused to leave Nobunaga's side. After defeating the Akechi troops, Yasuke would eventually be allowed safe passage back home to Africa.

The Story of Amina

This is a woman that captured the people's interest in every way. The young girl was born around 1533 in Zaria, Nigeria. Princess Amina was no ordinary girl. She came from a wealthy family, which possessed leather goods, fine clothing, salt, horses, and metals that were traded in her mother's Kingdom. After the princess' mother passed away, Amina waited ten years for her brother Karma's rule to end. She also had a sister that remains unknown, due to her choice to run away from Zaria. Although her mother is remembered for peace and great riches, Amina chose to focus on sharpening her military skills. She used her soldiers for training and mirrored their moves in battle. They were a skilled people that made metal gear to protect the soldiers' chest, arms, legs, and heads. The clever princess eventually built a sturdy wall, packed with dirt to keep the empire from outside attacks on her village. Amina chose not to get married, or to have children. She was a fearless warrior who couldn't be tamed or frightened away from any battle. Myths say the fictional story, "Xena Warrior Princess" existed because of Princess Amina and her powerful rule over lands.

The Story of Antar the Arabian Negro Warrior

Emerging from the intermarriage of an Arabian chief named Shedad and a slave mother named Zebiba, a baby boy named Antar was born. Antar's parents had traveled from place to place on a journey to build their empire. After Zebiba gave birth to Antar, one of her two sons, in a field, she had no idea how grand her little son would become. Though there's no known date of birth, Antar was said to be born around the 6th century in his time. As a boy, he was a keeper of camels, but his courage, physical strength, and sympathy for the weak excited the beautiful neighboring empires. Princess Ibla, daughter of King Malek, and Antar formed a union after Antar's undying love for lbla won him the princess. Soon, no longer was Antar a keeper of camels. Instead, he now trained with those considered first-class among fighting men. He was handpicked and trained by a great chieftain endowed with military qualities, poetic gifts, and a talent for leadership of extraordinary order. His deeds of heroism increased his popularity and ranks. After the death of his father, Antar became the protector of his tribe and the role model for Arabian and Negro gentlemen alike with his acts of chivalry. Since Antar possessed honorable and courteous behavior, the young chief inherited the responsibilities as the father of knighthood and the champion of the weak and oppressed, while being the protector of women.

The Story of Yaa Asantewaa

Yaa Asantewaa was a princess and mother of the Ejisu tribe. Her empire was called Ashanti, but today it is known as Ghana. In 1900 B.C., Yaa Asantewaa led her army into battle against the British colony. The great power of melanin that she possessed allowed Yaa Asantewaa to foresee dangers during tragic events that would occur. The princess saved her empire from many life-threatening events. She stood strong in what she believed in. There was a time in history when Yaa Asantewaa said, "If the men won't fight, I will take matters of war into my own hands." And she did, gathering her women up to fight for the safety of their land. The princess faced one of the most famous battles in history, in 1900 B.C., against the British. Although her melanin powers did not save her from being captured and sent her into exile to Seychelles, Yaa Asantewaa's bravery and incredible view into the future, led her to be honored, with schools being named after her. The great princess will forever be remembered for her brave uprising against the British and colonization.

The Story of Shaka Zulu

Nandi gave birth to a son named Shaka in 1787, but in order to prepare the prince with the skills to control an army and protect him from jealous family members, Nandi went into hiding. Shaka Zulu did not understand why he had to leave his homeland at a young age, but he would soon find out the truth. While Prince Shaka was away from the Kingdom, he trained very hard. One day, he returned home with his mother, ready to take his place on the throne of his Kingdom. In 1816, Shaka Zulu started out with around 1500 people in his tribe. He grew his tribe to over 250,000 members by attacking his enemies with long blades, and organizing military men. Unfortunately, when Shaka Zulu's Mother died in 1827, the prince was overcome with grief and sorrow. He had become a leader that the people feared more than they loved. He went from building up a Zulu nation to the destruction of his kingdom. He would lose his kingdom as a result of his overwhelming mourning of his mother. His courage and bravery will never be forgotten.

The Story of Nzinga Mbande

How do we begin this story about a princess who had to become a queen, not only to save a crown but her country of Ndongo, now known as Angola? Before earning the crown, her brother became king and sent Nzinga to negotiate with Portugal. The Portuguese were slave traders threatening their lands. It is said in many stories that at this meeting there was only one chair in the room when Nzinga arrived, and the governor sat in it. What the discourteous host didn't expect was for a beautiful woman to fall on her hands and knees to form a seat for the princess. Now that the princess had the governor at eye level, she would be able to use her brilliance and melanin that all black women possess, in defense of her people. Her leadership was proven worthy among her countries' enemies, and the peace treaty would be signed. But as our story shows, the Portuguese did not honor the treaty, and because of the heartbreak and suffering of his people, the King, her brother, died of sudden illness. Refusing the same fate as her brother, Nzinga went to war with Portugal and made sure everyone knew Angola was a land of the free and there would be no slaves coming from its shores. If there was ever a woman compared to the young Prince Hannibal, it would have to be Nzinga. Her trained warriors fought the Portuguese without fear. Even when it looked like she would be captured, her warriors made sure she had the land of the Matamba, in Angola. She continued to build her army and relentlessly fought the enemies of her country.

PART TWO

Great Melanated Heroes & Sheroes in the United States from the 17th Century to Present Times

The Story of Toussaint Louverture

If there was anyone that the United States of America owed a great deal of debt to, it would be Prince Toussaint Louverture and the people of Saint-Domingue, now called Haiti. In 1791, enslaved Africans in the country started a rebellion. Within a few years, Prince Toussaint had 800,000 enslaved Africans willing to die for freedom, justice, and equality. Trained to not only know his men, but also his allies and enemies, Prince Toussaint motivated his men to defeat the two most powerful armies ever assembled on two fronts (the British and the Spanish). He also changed history by defeating Napoleon and France, so aggressively that he claimed Napoleon's name and became known as the Black Napoleon. The only thing Napoleon and France could do was ask Toussaint for a peace treaty. During the meeting about the treaty, Napoleon's brother-in-law received orders by Napoleon to capture Prince Toussaint and bring him back to France. This cowardly act would surely change American history. What the world didn't know is that the prince's second-in-command General Jean-Jacques Dessalines already received his orders from the prince before he was betrayed by France. For the next five months after the prince was captured, Haiti damaged France and its military so drastically that in 1803, the Louisiana Purchase had to be made. The United States was able to buy 15 of its states for what some people bought a house for, because France didn't have the manpower or military strength to protect its shores and still occupy half of the United States' 828,000 square miles of land west of the Mississippi River. This story is just another great example of the contribution the blood of slaves has contributed to the American people.

The Story of Bass Reeves

Prince Bass Reeves was born a slave in Crawford County, Arkansas in 1838. He was named after his grandfather, Basse Washington. As a slave, he was owned by a man named William Reeves who was a politician and farmer. This young prince eventually became the main companion for Mr. Reeves' son, George. During the Civil War, Prince Bass realized his worth as a man and a leader and left the company of George Reeves because of a disagreement; and he became a fugitive because he was still the property of William Reeves. During this time, Bass hid out in the woods with indigenous people. Indigenous people are original people of a specific land. He trained with the Seminole, Cherokee, and Creek Indigenous people. He learned the language of each tribe he encountered. In 1863, the Emancipation Proclamation was signed, and Prince Bass was no longer a fugitive. With his freedom came very well-developed marksman skills. His skills were so great that he was banned from all gun competitions. People said it wouldn't be a fair competition if he were in it, because he was too good of a shooter. This was probably why Judge Parker had deputized Bass as a United States Marshal in 1875. Prince Bass was the first black man to become a United States Marshal. Deputy Marshal Bass Reeves served with the United States Marshal for 32 years. During this time, outlaws would tremble with fear when they heard Bass Reeves was after them. They knew that their chances of being caught were very high. He arrested 3,500 criminals during his career. Prince Bass was so dedicated to his career that he even arrested his own son for murder. Bass was a legend long after his career ended. It is common knowledge in Hollywood that "The Lone Ranger," a television series that aired on American Broadcasting Network, or ABC from 1949 to 1957 was based on the life and times of Bass Reeves.

The Story of Madam C.J. Walker

Sarah Breedlove was born in 1867 on a cotton plantation in Louisiana to parents who were recently set free from slavery. As a little girl, she picked cotton in harsh conditions, and at age 14 she married a man named Moses McWilliams. Just two years later, her husband died, and she moved to St. Louis. She attended night school, whenever she could. While in St. Louis, she married her second husband, Charles J. Walker, who would later help her promote her hair care business. In the 1890s, Sarah developed a scalp disorder that caused her to lose her hair. Like a scientist, she experimented with home remedies to improve her scalp condition and to make her hair grow. Her husband Charles helped her create advertisements for her hair care treatments for black people. He encouraged her to change her name to something that would stand out: Madam C.J. Walker, the name that she would use for the rest of her life. In 1907, Walker and her husband traveled the Southern states talking about her hair products and presenting live demonstrations of her "Walker Method" to make hair grow. She used her own pomade that she created, brushes, and heated combs on volunteers to show how well they worked. As Walker became more successful, in 1908 she opened a factory to make her products, established a beauty school to train other women in her "Walker Method" as well as how to be trained sales beauticians. These sisters were known as Walker Agents in the black community. In 1919, she was the only owner of her business that she had built from the ground up, which was worth over $1,000,000. She is known as one of the first American women to be a self-made millionaire. If Madam C.J. Walker could accomplish this level of success, as a granddaughter of slaves in the early 1900s, imagine what you can do today!

The Story of Dr. Mae Jemison

A brilliant cluster of light was born on October 17th, 1956 in Decatur, Alabama. She was the youngest of three children. When she was 3-years-old, her family moved to Chicago, Illinois so the children could receive a better education. At school and in the library, she discovered her love for science, especially astronomy, or the study of space. She became a medical doctor and traveled all over the world to practice medicine and help others. She helped at a summer refugee camp in Cambodia and also studied in Kenya. Then she decided to pursue her goal of space travel because she had long dreamed of reaching for the stars! She applied for the National Aeronautics Space program to be an astronaut. She was accepted into the program and became the first African-American woman on a week-long journey to space in September of 1992. The space mission was named, "Mission of the Shuttle Endeavor" and after completing the mission, Jemison became the only African American woman to complete a successful joint U.S. and Japan space mission. Princess Mae went on to finish her missions and she eventually developed her own project, The Jemison Group, a technology research, and development company. The young lady persevered to achieve her dreams and she continues to share her love for science and space exploration.

The Story of George Washington Carver

In 1864, near the end of the United States Civil War, George Washington Carver was born to slaves in Missouri. He and his family were owned by a man named Moses Carver. A week after George was born, he was kidnapped by raiders, along with his sister and mother, from their farm in Missouri and sold in Kentucky. George was the only one found and returned to Missouri. The slave owner's wife, Susan, decided to raise and educate him and his brother James. That's when George discovered he had a profound love for nature and a burning desire for knowledge. He left the farm to attend school. Years later, he became the first black student at Iowa State and earned his Bachelor of Science degree. Then, in 1896, Booker T. Washington, Tuskegee Institute's principal, recruited Carver to operate the agricultural department. As an inventor and student of plants, he developed more than 300 uses for peanuts and 100 uses for sweet potatoes, and his research helped farmers in the South. He used his fame to spread knowledge about science for the rest of his life. This innovative brother gave the world a new view of nature. For this, he will never be forgotten.

The Story of Charles Drew

As the oldest of five children, Charles was born in 1904 and grew up in a close-knit family. His education began in public school. He earned an Arts degree from Amherst College in 1926. He became a medical doctor and surgeon after graduating from McGill University in Canada in 1933. After spending a short time at Howard University as a live-in surgeon, Charles teamed up with a coworker and published, "Banked Blood: A Study in Blood Preservation" in 1940, which applied to shipping dried blood plasma to France and England during World War II. (Blood plasma is the part of blood that doesn't contain cells. Plasma can be stored longer than whole blood and used later to help people.) He became a director for the "Blood for Britain" project and later worked with the first American Red Cross Bank. As a medical revolutionist, Drew chose not to separate blood based on the donors' skin color, because it was not important. Brother Drew was an inspirational teacher who married Minnie Lenore Robins on September 23, 1939. They had four children together. Before Drew passed away in 1950, the last 19 papers he wrote showed his many interests. One of his concerns was for African American/Black people and their place in science. He provided blood throughout the world while being one of the most influential African Americans in the world of surgery today. Doctor Drew wrote "While one must grant at once that extraordinary talent, great intellectual strength, and unusual opportunity are necessary to break out of this prison of the Negro

Problem. We believe that the Negro in the field of physical sciences has not only opened a small passageway to the outside world, but is carving a road in many untrod areas, along which later generations will find it easier to travel. The breaching of these laws and the laying of this road has not been, and is not easy."

The Story of Oprah Winfrey

The story of Oprah is one that lives in our hearts and not just in books. It began on a farm in Mississippi, in a town called Kosciusko. At 3-years-old, her grandmother taught her to read and speak in front of crowds. Young Oprah's mother, a maid, raised her for a few years until Oprah turned 14-years-old and was sent to live with her father in Tennessee. He instilled the power of focus and discipline in her. In high school, Oprah won prizes for oratory and dramatic recitation. She also won the Miss Black Tennessee beauty pageant. After high school, Oprah took her place as a role model in the Black community of Nashville. She became a well-known personality at a local radio station. She earned a full scholarship to Tennessee State University. She combined her education and fearlessness and took the world by storm! She started out as a princess, but it wasn't long before she became a queen with an epic empire. In 1988, she became the youngest person to win the Radio and Television Society's "Broadcaster of the Year" Award. She started her own production company called Harpo Productions and became the first woman to produce her own television show, "The Oprah Winfrey Show." She became part owner of the Oxygen Television Network and currently owns OWN Television Network. She's responsible for getting the Oprah Bill, also known as the National Child Protection Act passed by President Bill Clinton in 1993 and she received the Medal of Freedom by President Barack Obama in 2013. She opened a school for young girls in South Africa and does her best to ensure that the students at her school also receive a college education. Oprah, who was once a young aspiring sister, is now a self-made billionaire who shares her wealth, knowledge, and wisdom all over the world. And that is why the young people are asking the Ancestors for her Presidency in 2020.

The Story of Muhammad Ali

All it took was a bully stealing this young brother's bike to activate the ancestral bloodline of greatness he was born with. The police officer that the young Cassius Clay reported his bike being stolen to, eventually would be the same man who would train him and see that he never got bullied again. Officer Martin had never seen a 12-year-old work so hard and train so much. Every morning the young Cassius raced the school bus to campus; and he ate healthy every day. It didn't take long for him to have to put his training on display. By the time young Cassius had turned 18, he had become a six-time National Golden Gloves champion and won the Gold Medal at the 1960 Olympic Games by defeating a fighter from Poland. The brother became an American hero when he won a match against British heavyweight champion, Mr. Cooper, in 1963; and then knocked out Sonny Liston in 1964 to become heavyweight champion of the world. His famous phrase was, "Float like a butterfly, sting like a bee." The next day, the young Cassius announced he would now be called Muhammad Ali, after talking with his teacher, The Honorable Elijah Muhammad. In 1967, Muhammad Ali refused military induction for the Vietnam War because he was a humanitarian. As a result, the U.S. government put him in jail and banned him from boxing for over three years. In 1971, he won his appeal and was exonerated. In 1974, in Africa, he got his title back in front of 60,000 Africans at Rumble in the Jungle, beating the undefeated champion, George Foreman. But the greatest fight he fought came a year later in the Philippines, "Thrilla in Manila." It was Muhammad Ali and Joe Frazier in the final boxing match to see who was the greatest. Muhammad Ali was victorious again. Three years later, he faced another championship rematch in New Orleans, Louisiana against the champion Leon Spinks. Muhammad not only won, but was the only heavyweight to win the title three times. Muhammad Ali is not just one of our greatest sports figures of the 20th century, but also one of the greatest humanitarians.

The Story of Serena and Venus Williams

There is royalty in our society that was born and bred in Compton, California. Venus and Serena Williams are proof of that. These two sisters bring new meaning to the word champions! Venus and Serena are the youngest of nine children. Serena Williams was born in 1981, and her older sister, Venus, was born in 1980 to their parents, Richard and Oracene. Their father started to train them in tennis at very young ages. He was stern and kept the girls focused on being good students and excellent tennis players. He wanted them to surpass any expectation that they may have had of themselves. Compton was not only their home, but it was their training ground in life. With the mastery of their sport, they had to learn how to overpower any opponent on the tennis court, no matter how good they were. This exemplary way of playing tennis led to the melanated beauties making history. They are the only two sisters in history to be ranked 1 and 2 in the tennis world. Not to mention, these majestic beauties have four Olympic Gold medals each, as well as 29 Grand Slam titles. They have also done well in business. They are both part owners of the Miami Dolphins, an NFL football team, and they have built several schools in Africa. People of African descent all over the world are honored by the two sisters' success. Closing Thoughts: We would like to Congratulate Serena and Alexis Ohanian for the birth of little princess Alexis Olympia Ohanian Jr, their Bundle Of Joy.

The Story of Nick Cannon

Nick Cannon was a birth the Ancestors gave to a village in southeastern San Diego, called Lincoln Park. Although this young brother never got involved with the wars in the streets his community was connected to, he still felt the pain in the loss of life, growing up. His grandfather taught him his bloodline and what he was destined to become. His father trained him and helped the young Nick master his craft. Nothing inspired him more than showing not just his friends, but the world, that growing up in the trenches only makes your dreams clearer; never give up on them. At 17-years-old, he became the youngest staff writer in television history. From there, Nick acted, produced and directed. In 2002, he captivated the world with his first lead role in the movie "Drumline." Not stopping there, Nick released his Hip Hop album in 2003 that hit the charts and billboards. He was asked to return to the movie screen. So, for the next three years, young Nick did what he was trained to do: make the people and Ancestors proud. In 2007, he made history again by being the first African American to be honored with the Breakthrough Actor/Performer of the Year award at the Cannes Film Festival. In 2008, Nick fell in love with Mariah Carey. In 2011, Mariah gave birth to twins: A boy and a girl, Moroccan and Monroe. Though Nick and Mariah divorced, they continued to co-parent. A few years later, Nick was honored with another son by the name of Golden who will surely inherit the benefits of his father's success and guidance.

The Story of Colin Kaepernick

This remarkable young man was born on November 3, 1978 in Milwaukee, Wisconsin to a very young mother. She made the brave decision to give baby Colin up for adoption to a white family, where he has an older brother and sister. When Colin was 4 years old, the Kaepernicks moved to California and when he was 8, he started playing football. With his strong arm, he took the position of quarterback on his team. In fourth grade, young Colin wrote a letter, hoping to go to a good college and then to play in the professional football league for the 49ers or the Packers. Not only was Colin an incredibly talented athlete, he was also highly intelligent. He graduated with a 4.0 from the University of Nevada, Reno; and then his wish became reality when he was drafted by the San Francisco 49ers in 2011. Just a year later, Kaepernick became the starting quarterback and led the team to the Super Bowl. Kaepernick did something very brave in August 2016 – he refused to stand for the national anthem, in order to call attention to racial injustice, police brutality and the nation's cultural divide. He explained "I am not going to stand up to show pride in a flag for a country that oppresses black people and people of color. To me, this is bigger than football, and it would be selfish on my part to look the other way. There are bodies in the street and people getting paid leave and getting away with murder". Those were some powerful words and he embraced the warrior's mentality of his great elder Muhammad Ali, who once had to stand on those same principles. At the end of the football season, Kaepernick became a player without a team. The brave man filed a grievance in October 2017 against the owners of the NFL for collusion, and his exclusion of the football league. Despite negative comments and media, young Colin and his courageous actions earned him the title, "Citizen of the Year" from GQ Magazine, Sports Illustrated awarded him the "Muhammad Ali Legacy Award" and he was runner up for the TIME magazines' "Person of the Year". Closing Thoughts. We would like to salute the players who continued to kneel in solidarity with Colin in his efforts to spread awareness: Eric Reid, Marshawn Lynch, Kenny Stills, Michael Thomas and Julius Thomas.

The Story of Marilyn Mosby

Marilyn Mosby came from five generations of police officers and was the first of her family to graduate from college. After college, she graduated from Boston College Law School, worked as Assistant State's Attorney for Baltimore, and afterward as an insurance agent. In 2015, Marilyn announced her decision to run for State's Attorney for the city of Baltimore, and she won! This made Marilyn Mosby the youngest prosecutor in the United States. The fired-up young Marilyn promised to keep bad guys off the streets and began a program to prevent drugs from destroying the black people's neighborhoods. What makes Marilyn Mosby so incredible was her bold choice to charge six police officers with murder. She fought for justice on behalf of a young 25-year-old black man named Freddie Gray, whose neck was brutally broken. The young man died in 2015 due to an arrest made a week prior by the same six police officers. Marilyn's cousin was killed near her childhood home, after being mistaken for a drug dealer. Those are the stories that paint a different picture, and place officers on the wrong side of the law. As the case against the police officers leaves the nation uncertain, Marilyn Mosby showed unbelievable courage by standing up for what is right. The people remain hopeful and proud to have a strong Black woman as their State's Attorney when staring in the face of racial danger. Marilyn Mosby shows real courage by standing up for what's right. The people remain hopeful and proud to have a strong sister on their side in their fight for justice.

The Story of Aaron McGruder

Aaron was born in Chicago in 1974, but that would not be where his mind began to develop into the writer-producer and cartoonist we know today. It started after he and his family moved to Columbia, Maryland when he was 6-years-old. Young Aaron was in search of his purpose. His interest in knowledge fueled little Aaron's thirst for information and motivated him to never stop learning or seeking a higher education. Young Aaron went on to graduate from the University of Maryland with a degree in African Studies, where he challenged himself to think about living in America. He published comic books in his school's newspaper. A groundbreaking event, September 11, 2001, caused Aaron to break away from the regularly accepted comic strip and rebel against society. He called out the U.S. government and created some enemies along his journey as a cartoonist. Then he created "The Boondocks," a funny cartoon that touched on historical, political and cultural themes. He looked within himself to create a cartoon that young African American/Black people could be proud of. Not only because it shows two young brothers who try to copy heroes that came before him, but because it revealed an image that young men filled with melanin could relate to each other through laughter, and not resort to violence. Aaron also produced the movie, "Red Tails," and "The Tuskegee Airmen," which are also a part of Black history. Aaron continues to honor the ancestors by challenging African American/Black people to think, and he honors them daily by living out his dreams and purpose. Because of his brilliance and vigilance, the ancestors live on through his work.

The Story of Misty Copeland

Misty Copeland was born in beautiful Kansas City, Missouri in 1982. She later moved to San Pedro, Los Angeles where she grew up with her four siblings. Misty was the youngest of her siblings and was filled with spunk and charisma. She was born with a special gift of melanin and rhythm in her ancestral bloodline. Naturally graceful and classical, Misty started ballerina lessons when she was 13-years old. By the age of 15, she was an advanced dancer who had excelled in her skills. She won first place at the Music Center Spotlight Awards. She has gone on to become the first young Black woman to be promoted as a principal dancer at the American Ballet Theater. She's performed in several pieces, including: The Nutcracker, Swan Lake, and Romeo & Juliet. In addition, she's dedicated her efforts to help youth-based organizations. President Barack Obama chose her to be a distinguished member of the President's Council on Fitness, Sports, and Nutrition in 2014. Misty also authored a New York Times Bestselling book called, "Life in Motion". Misty Copeland inspires countless people around the world.

The Story of Beyoncé Knowles

On the 4th day of September 1981 the Ancestors saw a need in Houston, TX. That need was filled in the form of a princess, young Beyoncé Giselle Knowles. Early in life, Beyoncé's father and mother Matthew and Tina saw amazing potential in Beyoncé's entertainment abilities. It wasn't long after that she began performing at shows and getting herself known. In the late 90's she and other talented young princesses were the hottest female group, Destiny's Child. From there, Beyoncé went solo and eventually took control of her own management. She married Jay-Z, a well-known artist, millionaire, and field general in the cause for the freedom of speech. They have three beautiful children: Princess Blue Ivy and twins Prince Sir and Princess Rumi. Other accolades of Beyoncé' include 22 Grammy awards, most nominated woman in Grammy history, MTV VMA awards, and many others. Around the world, many cultures and age groups of people thank our Ancestors for blessing the world with Mrs. Queen Bee.

The Story of Simone Biles

Young Simone Biles was born in 1997 in Columbus, Ohio and would flip onto the scene in 2003. Her mother struggled with problems in life, which caused her to give her children up for adoption. This type of change in Simone's life made her understand how to deal with the pressures of leadership. She lived with her grandparents, along with one of her sisters, Adria. The other two siblings lived with another close family member. Simone loved gymnastics so much that she decided to home school, so she could train for her sport. She even had the chance to go to college, but decided to take a chance of a lifetime and, instead, pursue gymnastics. The understanding that college was always a place she could go back to in the future caused Simone Biles to pursue her gymnastics career. She won 14 World Championship gold medals from 2013-2016 and became a five-time Olympic medalist in 2016. The young lady gained so much popularity that she was offered many deals to promote products, due to her beautiful smile and charm.

The Story of Michelle Obama

Michelle LaVaughn Robinson, also known as Michelle Obama was born with a mission that would please the ancestors. She was raised on Chicago's South Side, one of the toughest neighborhoods in the United States of America. Her upbringing gave her the hands-on experience needed to balance the heavy load the universe would entrust in her. She was also blessed with parents that took drastic measures to ensure she was a success. Young Michelle traveled miles from home to attend Whitney M. Young Magnet High School, where she was an active and productive student. She became the student council treasurer and graduated class Salutatorian in 1981. Then she attended Princeton University with her brother, Craig, where she created a children's reading program for the children of the school's manual laborers. After graduating with honors, she moved onto Harvard University where the needs of the people and her goals became very clear. She decided to obtain her doctoral degree in law and began practicing law. Then, because of her excellence, she was tasked with mentoring a colleague named Barack Hussein Obama. She became Barack's greatest ally and biggest supporter, and eventually, his wife. She exemplified the phrase "behind every strong man is an even stronger woman." She had a public service track record that took her from the front lines, working hands-on with the poor and underserved, to various positions at the mayor's office. Her vast experience helped to build relationships with good people that would help Brother Barack in his political career. The couple had two beautiful daughters, Sasha and Malia. They inspired Barack and Michelle to want the country to progress in a way that would make the world a better place, not only for their children, but for all children. Michelle, who was growing into a beautiful Black woman supported her husband right into a seat in the United States Senate; and later, as he became the first black man to win the office of President of the United States. She became the first Black First Lady of the United States and an inspiration for nations around the world.

The Story of Barack Obama

Barack Obama, the first African-American President of the United States was born in 1961 in Honolulu, Hawaii. His mother was named Ann Dunham, and his father, who was Nigerian, was Barack Obama, Sr. Unfortunately, Barack parted ways from his father when his parents divorced each other, when Barack was a toddler. His mother remarried and moved to Jakarta, Indonesia, a year later. Scary events in Indonesia forced his mother to send 10-year-old Barack back to his grandparents in Hawaii for safety. He flourished while living with his grandparents. They enrolled him in high school where he played basketball and graduated with honors. But his absent father left him longing for a father-figure and answers about his ancestors. Sadly, this led Barack to later refer to his father as a man who remained a myth. Still, Barack had a calling to help people, early on in life. He knew he needed more education to become an effective leader. He graduated from Columbia University in 1983, and then attended Harvard, the same school his father had attended, to study law. After graduation, he knew he needed to be someplace where he could make a difference. The brother made a life changing decision in 1985 and moved to Chicago to practice law. At the Sidney Austin Law Firm in Chicago, he also worked under the mentorship of his future wife, Michelle. She later became his best friend, his wife, and the mother of his two daughters, Sasha and Malia. He became a state senator while living in Chicago. Then he decided to run for President of the United

States of America. In November 2008, Obama became the first African-American President of the United States. He served two terms as President, where he reformed health care, changed immigration laws and gave the black community a sense of pride that it has never had. President Barack Obama has gone back into life as a private citizen but his powerful, peaceful legacy remains in the memories of people all over the world.

PART THREE

We are Our Ancestors' Keepers: "Knowledge is Power" Quiz

Test Your Knowledge, Write your Answers Below:

1. Who refused to stand for the national anthem to raise awareness to police brutality? _____

2. What person spent 34 years commanding an army and growing a kingdom to become the greatest empire there ever existed in history? _____

3. Who published their first cartoon in their college newspaper? _____

4. Who had to escape from Egypt to Syria to escape death? _____

5. Which princess sat equally to her husband on the throne during their Egyptian rule? _____

6. Which princess defeated Alexander the Great? _____

7. She saved their empire from many life-threatening events, due to seeing into the future. _____

8. Who experimented with home remedies to improve her scalp condition and to make her hair grow? _____

9. King Solomon built an apartment for her stay at his empire. _____

10. Who was banned from any competition because of their ability to shoot guns with both hands? _____

11. Who became the protector of his tribe when his father died? _____

12. Who is said to have had the strength greater than 10 men? _____

13. Whose military tactics are still being studied in many schools today? _____

14. Who had fun working with the elders as they taught him the ways of the past? _____

15. Who had the richest empire in the world? _____

16. Who is recorded as the world's first multi-genius? _____

17. Who attended Princeton University with her brother? _____

18. Who was the brilliant cluster of light? _____

19. Who married a well-known field general? _____

20. Who became a five-time Olympic medalist in 2016? _____

21. Who did Booker T. Washington recruit to operate the agricultural department at Tuskegee Institute? _____

22. Two African American sisters who have played tennis since they were children, what are their names? _____

23. Who came from five generations of police officers? _____

24. Who helped create the blood bank, and were concerned about science and African Americans? _____

25. This ruler was overcome by grief from his mothers' death. What is his name? _____

26. Which famous boxer said the popular words "Float like a butterfly, sting like a bee?" _____

27. Who was the 44th President of the United States? _____

28. An African American/Black daytime television host that opened up a school in Africa. _____

29. Legend has it that, 'Xena Warrior Princess' was named after this woman. _____

30. Who was the man responsible for doubling the size of the United States? _____

31. Who became the youngest staff writer in television history?
_____

32. Who made history in 75 years of Ballet? _____

1. Colin Kaepernick

2. Amina

3. Aaron McGruder

4. Cleopatra

5. Nefertiti

6. Candace

7. Yaa Asantewaa

8. Madam C.J. Walker

9. Makeda

10. Bass Reeves

11. Antar

12. Yasuke Oda Nobunaga

13. Hannibal

14. Alfonso

15. Mansa Musa

16. Imhotep

17. Michelle Obama

18. Mae Jemison

19. Beyoncé Knowles

20. Simone Biles

21. George Washington Carver

22. Williams Sisters

23. Marilyn Mosby

24. Charles Drew

25. Shaka Zulu

26. Muhammad Ali

27. Barack Obama

28. Oprah Winfrey

29. Nzinga

30. Toussiant Louverture

31. Nick Cannon

32. Misty Copeland

Acknowledgements

First and foremost, I would like to thank The Almighty, my grandmother, Mary Gotell, my mother, Rita Gotell, The Honorable Minister Louis Farrakhan & Mother Khadijah, Ky'Lah Tucker, Brother Stu and the rest of my family. Next, I would like to thank Student Minister Hugh Muhammad & Sybila Elisah Muhammad, Pastor Terry Brooks, Pastor Reginald Gary, Pastor Rickey Laster, and Dr. John Warren, Pastor Wells. In addition, I would like to thank The Brotherhood & Sisterhood, Capt. David Muhammad, Black Men United, San Diego Voice & Viewpoint, San Diego Monitor News. Top Gun Entertainment, Gladiator School of Martial Arts and Boxing, Lincoln High School Cluster and Morse High School Cluster for always putting our children first.

A special thank you to The Healing5 Foundation, Inc. and www.theherbalcontainer.com,

Elite 8 would like to send Special Thanks To A Few Of The First Ladies Of San Diego California:

Mother Kathleen Harmon. Racquel Vasquez, the First African American Mayor in a city in San Diego County- Lemon Grove, California. Myrtle Cole, she is the First African American Councilwoman & Council President - 4th district. Dr. Shirley Webber, she is the First African American to be elected to office South of Los Angeles, Assembly-member 79th district.

Alpha Kappa Alpha Sorority, Inc.- Epsilon Xi Omega Chapter.

Chida Rebecca @ http://www.blackandmagazine.com.

My Sister from Nigeria, Ifafunke Oladigbolu @ www.lolasafricanapparel.com.

Please Be On The Lookout For My Beautiful Sister's Book!!!
Love Incorruptible: A Woman's Reflective Journey to Freedom.
bit.ly/jazminsteele

A very very special Thank You from the top of my heart to Sister Ciara! The first person to believe in both visions the Ancestors put within the soul of this Black Man for the people...100 reasons why Black Women should accept the Black Man's apology and We Are Our Ancestors' Keepers.

Thank you Nigel Binns, Sculptor of mother of humanity project & Elite 8 Akilah Shaheed

We also would like to thank Stephen Pierce, President of The NFL Players Association San Diego & President of The Stephen Pierce Foundation.

About the Author

Charles 3X Alexander is the Director of Outreach for "I Am My Brother's Keeper (IAMBK)." He was born and raised in the city of San Diego, California. He is most proud of his three children, Shei'Lece Tone, Osiris, and Chariah Alexander. He considers them his greatest gift and contribution to the world. Because of his many years involved with community organizations such as The Compassion Project, Black Men United, Together We Build, and his participation in co-founding Overcoming Gangs, an organization designed to help youth triumph over peer pressure, he has worked collectively and collaboratively with all stakeholders for the betterment of the community. He is also a football coach with the Balboa Raiders Youth Football and Cheer Organization. His expertise and insight have become invaluable to the IAMBK team.

He is responsible for several initiatives such as "Every Day is Mother's Day," mentoring and tutoring in local elementary schools, and assisting in a weekly free food program. His leadership has been instrumental in improving our communities' objectives to stop the unwarranted issuance of liquor licenses in inner city neighborhoods. For countless years, he petitioned city government officials to bring resources and summer food programs to the Mt. Hope Community, and it paid off in the summer of 2013. His hard work resulted in being awarded the Urban League's 40 and Under Award, NAACP Unsung Heroes Award.

He has played a critical role within San Diego County as a young up-and-coming leader. Charles has been featured in two local documentaries: MTV Flipped, and has collaborated with the students of Rancho Bernardo High School, which consecutively won first place and afforded the students' college admission into film school. In 2016, the San Diego Voice & Viewpoint honored him with the Community Activist Award. He received the 2017 BAPAC Community Activist Award. (BAPAC is the Black Political Association of California.) He's currently working on his latest project, a documentary, "100 Reasons Why Black Women Should Accept the Black Man's Apology." Charles Alexander continues to serve the community with his leadership skills and courage to stand on the frontline in the face of adversity.

www.ingramcontent.com/pod-product-compliance
Lightning Source LLC
Chambersburg PA
CBHW042355280426
43661CB00095B/1127